"Every great change is preceded by chaos."

- Deepak Chopra

A Note From Me

I have a message for you:

Never give up
You are not alone

Sometimes we bump into angels
They shake us awake and rattle our soul
Help us to settle the chaos surrounding
When the world seems to swallow us whole

If ever you find yourself hopeless
Needing a friend, alone, or defeated
I will be waiting inside of these pages
Here you'll find me, whenever I'm needed

Sit with me in the moment
Collecting words and spilling thoughts
Together, we'll conquer the chaos
Finding comfort that hope is not lost.

- Natalie

OUT OF CHAOS

by Natalie Nascenzi

PUBLISHING

ii Publishing
New York, NY

www.toniiinc.com

Cover design by tonii

ISBN: 978-0-578-64451-6

Unedited Diary Excerpt, 2018

"...and for years the anxious beast within me rumbled, at ease, going unnoticed. It slept in its cave. It wept in the shadows of my soul. But it remained at bay. The quiet hum of the sea silenced the madness. It wrapped the chaos tightly in a box with a bow and slid it beneath my rib cage. Tucked away. Always there but never unraveling. Until now. This loud, fast, world shook the box free, un-wedged it from my core and dumped the contents. My body tensed with fury, confusion, doubt. "What If's." And then, it consumed me. Wholly. Totally..."

And I found myself asking...

Who is She?

There is a stranger staring back at me
A ghost within a frame
I try to see myself in her
Yet
We only share a name

Frightening and peculiar
Her eyes the same as mine
But who she is
And who I am
Simply does not align

I touch my cheek
My nose
My eyes
Tug gently at my hair
I watch her mirror every move
Unable to break our stare

My eyes trail over her body
Studying her curves and her face
Frantic
I search for resemblance
But there is nothing
Not even a trace

"She is me and I am her"
Unconvincing
"I am her and she is me"
Can't be true
I want to see me when I look at her
But there's something evil obstructing my view

Distorting my gaze is a false sense of self
I cannot fathom that we are the same
Painful
Bewildered
Her beauty is mine
She is me
She is who I became

I weep for the girl who I used to be
As I lower her into her grave
Then I turn to the girl in the mirror
And say thank you
For being so brave.

For the Four

...and one more: My brother, Nathan.

"Never lose hope."

You, Me, and 33

INTO

CHAOS

1. The Ambivalent Amphibians

I am a creature
Who weaves false hopes with expectations
Dwelling intermediately
Victim of interpretations

Trapped by indecision
Choices, chains shackled to my ankles
A prisoner on uncertainty
A twisted rope
Left in tangles

The Ambivalent Amphibian
Lurking in bottomless, muddy waters
An endless mind of chaos
One which never falters

Trying to stay above
But these chains pull me
Down
Down
Down
These chains they pull me downward
Reluctantly
I drown

Sinking slowly into darkness
Abyss traps me like a cage
These heavy chains around my ankles
This all-consuming rage
Swim upwards screams the silence
Break free
Control your kind!

But this creature knows no such feeling
Held captive by the mind

These beasts they juggle odds
Over contemplate the outcome
They toss and turn with choices
The chains
They can't escape from

And I
The wicked master
Of this distraught, unruly race
Sinking slowly to the bottom
I disappear without a trace.

2. The Monster

My chaotic mind on fire
Fighting an angry beast within
There's gunshots
Explosions
Smoke and dust
I fear
I may not win

Twisted up in fear and shame
It fills my lungs
I choke
Yet, something keeps me fighting
The mental monster
I've provoked

I resist against the turmoil
To its greatest satisfaction
Resistance feeds its spirit
Its guilty pleasure
My reaction

My soul screams back in anguish
"Please don't believe these lies!"
As the monster taunts and fools me
It longs for my demise

I push
It pulls
I protest

It lingers in my mind
Laughing at its victory
Wicked
Cruel
Unkind

But little does this monster know
My soul is that much stronger
And every time it makes me fall
I rise again
I prosper

My truest self, it conquers
Logic floods my veins
The monster loses power
And I
I take the reins

The smoke
It finally settles
My mind begins to clear
"The monster was myself!"
I cry
"The monster was my fear"

A tear falls down my cheek
Drips slowly to my chin
The inner beast has lost its grip
And I
Begin again

The chaos turns to silence
The battle nears its end
The monster
Once an enemy
Now becomes my friend.

3. Repetitive Chaos

Repetitive chaos of the mind
Some would say
Insane
Insane
Insane
A twisted mess of racing thoughts
An apocalyptic brain

I say to myself
"No, not this time
You've walked this road before"
But my mind pulls me back into chaos
My logic, too easily ignored

Unable to step into elsewhere
I dance on the edge of my madness
Madness
Madness
Unable to break the cycle
To escape from the chains of this mad mess

I repeat
Over and over again
Order
Formation
My sanity
Seems impossible to ever obtain

Craving the stillness of silence
Longing for peace of the mind
How can this chaos control me?
It has no meaning
It lives undefined

Yet it lingers and pulls me in deeper
Down into the depths of the sea
It drags me down
Deeper and deeper
Until it's just me
Face to face with my reaper

On the inside I scream
"Don't look through me
Leave me be
These are my own affairs!"
Hiding my face from thousands of eyes
Slowly burning in the flames of their stares

On repeat
Repeat
Repeat
Searching for the strength
Resisting defeat
This mind on repeat
Repeating

It has no meaning
No meaning
No meaning
Repetitive mind

Undefined
No, not this time

Please don't consume me.

4. Nicotine Lust

Burn my throat
Make me choke
Feed my madness
Set fire to my lungs
Hot tar and ashes

Linger in my mouth
Fill the air
Fuel my mental
Every pull
Every puff
Feels transcendental

Contaminate my taste buds
Make my spit thick
And black
And foul
Inhale as I shake my head
A cringe
A sigh
I scowl

Yet I pull
Harder
Longer
Deeper
Until I choke on the smoke
My throat aches
I understand that it's simply an addiction
It's earned its place on my list of mistakes

Oh
Foul odor, fill my nose
Make me breathless
Make me light in the head
Giddy, high

Make me wish that I never picked you up at all
"Putting you down is too impossible," I sigh

I hold my breath
Look away and I ponder
Shake my head
Slowly smile
My release
Then I smash the cherry embers in the ash tray
And my insanity fizzles out into peace

I watch the smoke trail up from the ashes
It billows from a grave of butts and dust
Filling the silence of the air all around me
My greatest weakness
Guilty pleasure

Nicotine lust.

5. Not Me

If you told me
I'd be here
A fugitive of my thoughts
A wandering Neanderthal on an unknown quest
A restless jumble of skin and bone
A universe of chaos
I'd've laughed
Not me

If you told me
I'd be trapizing from one moment to another
Fearing each swing that I'd lose my grasp
Then come crashing back down to earth
I'd've laughed
Not me

If you told me
I'd run blindly
Head-first into the storm
Lasso the eye
And drag it silently behind me
Told me I'd walk through the world glass-eyed
Mind racing
Fists balled tightly at my sides...

I'd've laughed
Not me
Not me
Not me

I am a laugher
A lover
A flower swaying gently in the breeze
Watching death pass by
Praying please
Don't pick me

I am still blooming.

6. Drowning in Cotton

I laid in bed with tears in my eyes
In a frenzy of twists and turns
Spinning and flipping along with a mind
Full of worry
Anxiety
Concerns

I buried my face in my pillow
I choked on my breath as I wept
Too nice
Too trusting
I cry to myself
Not good enough
Worthless
Inept

I tangled myself in the blankets
Drowning in cotton, I cried
Behind me, a closet of monsters
But I have nowhere to hide

I danced in my sheets in frustration
A restless
Sleepless waltz
Wide eyed and awake
Over thinking
My fears
My issues
My faults

I closed my eyes and prayed
A voice whispered
"It will all be okay"
God gave me hug
I drifted to sleep
Knowing tomorrow is a brand new day.

7. Path of Sun

Airbrushing the sky as it peeks its eyes
Over a blazing horizon
Showering the earth with shades of gold
This is a new sun rising

Awakening the world with its brilliance
Announcing "new day!" with a lustrous glow
Kissing the landscape with radiance
Nature's most captivating show

Delicately gracing the ocean
Light as a feather
A gentle caress
A glistening line growing slowly with time
An incandescent, glorious bliss

Slowly unrolling before me
A carpet of light
Threaded with beams
Tassels of gold from the finest of twine
Woven with glistening seams

Stitched with the fabric of fantasy
Sparkling
Dazzling
Bright
Painting the heavens with yellows and pinks
A waterfall
Cascading with light

This glittering path gleams before me
A shimmering aisle of gold
Holding its shape above water
As a new day begins to unfold

This liquid invitation before me
Leading me into the sun
An avenue of diamonds
The walkway to heaven

Spectacular
A new day has begun.

8. The Fleeting Meteorite

I am as fleeting as a meteorite
A comet dancing across your sky
And only for a moment
I am the moon, I rise with the tides

I illuminate the landscape
I'm a swift wind beneath the sail
I crash with the waves and fall with the leaves
The perfect balance of an uneven scale

I'm short, unpredictable seasons
Like lightening
I flash then I strike
My current is quick and electrifying
A free bird
I swoop in
Then take flight

Yet
A shadow of doubt walks beside me
It's the glue that keeps me in place
Disguising itself as a compass
A mask clinging tight to my face

Binding
Relentless
It holds me

But my mind on a quest to break free
Is that of a prey to a predator
My instincts step in
And I flee

Those who cross my path try to grasp me
But I fall through their fingers like sand

"I'm sorry, I'm a firework, not a bonfire"

This restless life
They do not understand

An impossible task to stay grounded
To stay still and confined to one space
Because I am as fleeting as a meteorite
In a universe that never takes shape.

9. The Inverted City

Two people

The upside down city, their playground
A world that dazzles beneath their feet

Wandering souls
Two minds stuck in time
Drifting aimless
Unexpected
They meet

Enthralled with the chaos of street lights
A mess of buildings crafted from glass
They shatter the world with their presence
And watch as the structures collapse

Concrete crumbles to the ground around them
A peaceful whirlwind of dust and debris
The inverted city of silence
Of stillness, calmness, and ease

Finally, she reads

Drifting upward from darkness toward freedom
Breaking surface and gasping for air
Greeted by a galaxy of twinkling lights
From the upside down city, stripped bare

A chaotic mind on fire
A fountain that douses the flames
The amphibian-of-ambivalence dances in bliss
Finally, free from her chains

The city flips and it spins
And with it they danced
Entranced by outlines left behind
Surrounded by sonder on Park
Enchanted
Two souls
Now entwined.

10. The Rains Atlas

Caught in a flurry of my own wishful thinking
A light sprinkle of scattering thoughts
They rain down and gather around me
Unsure which to choose
I cast lots

But even with chance
I question each choice
Every thought becomes a challenge
I wobble the tightrope of decision
Unfortunately
Losing my balance

Unsure
The downpour
Continues

The droplets fashion themselves into paper
They collect and form into a map
But with too many points on this atlas
I stand frozen
Unable to act

Searching for solace and answers
Too weary to grasp a direction
Pinned to the wall
In front of this map
Now a hostage of impending selection

I desire each destination
Grapple with which route to follow
I picture each outcome
Unable to choose
And so
In my choices
I wallow

Time passes as I sit with this crisis
The rain accumulates into a sea
And now, my mind

The lost sailor
Stranded
With a map I can't read

Drifting in an ocean of options
Approaching a waterfall into abyss
With not much time
I must make a choice
Yet, I stare out at the void
Motionless

The edge creeps up
I panic
Blinded by droplets of doubt
Under these storm clouds of conflict
I cower
In the face of uncertainty
I blackout

Suddenly
Clarity
It strikes me
Just as the boat starts to tip
Jolted by my own intuition
With the shoreline in sight

I jump ship.

11. The Duality of Selves

You, me, and our conflicting selves
Locked in a room, confused
Tasked with the pleasure of piecing together
A puzzle
We sit there, bemused

This puzzle of innumerable pieces
Multifarious shapes out of place
Strewn on the ground all around us
Bewildered, we sit, face to face

Trying to work out the image
But our selves do not see it the same
Our unmatched perspective perplexes us
Befuddled, we sit there, in vain

Given a task so simple to most
Becomes a battle of both perceptions
Two selves, unaligned, search the pieces
Baffled, by our own apprehensions

This fragmented image
Undeveloped
Scattered in every direction
One by one, we pick up each piece
And arrange them section by section

Casting aside our own inputs
Putting each piece into place
The image comes slowly together
Now in sync, here we sit, interlaced

Building and building and building
But will eternally remain incomplete
This puzzle before us
Forever unfinished

Two selves
And one missing piece.

12. Blocked

I am blank and empty
It's the writers greatest fear
Staring at sheets of paper
But the words do not appear

The lack of inspiration
Begins to take its toll
And although I try to fight it
It's out of my control

Pen to paper
Hand to head
Eyes burning with frustration
Scribbling
Ripping
Crossing out
Fingers tapping with impatience

Trying to find the words
But they float up, up
And away
Far from the paper in front of me
These words
How they've betrayed

Some say
"Oh it's just writers block
It comes and goes in waves"
But without my release
I am lost at sea
And writing is what saves

I question all my sentences
Every syllable
Every line
But nothing seems to flow quite right
Like me
They don't align

Crumpled up papers litter the floor
Fallen words sit idle at my feet
A pile of literary misfits
Each one, a relic of defeat

"Everything sounds the same," I sigh
"It all just sounds so blah!"
"Call it a day!"
"Throw in the towel!"
Abruptly
I'm struck with "AH HA!"

So it goes
The process begins
My fingers can barely keep pace
The writer's block crumbles to dust

And

                                             All

                                    The

                           Words

                  Fall

            Into

Place.

13. World of Fake Roses

We live in a world of fake roses
At first glance, their beauty unmatched
Yet the closer you get, the more you will see
A deception so clear and unmasked

A plastic exterior
Stealing your gaze
Spreading rapidly
Like airborne disease

Creating a meadow of false perception
This world we live
In which beauty deceives

Shallow roots plague the soil
Choking the earth
Scentless, senseless, and crude

Reflecting the sun
Never soaking it in
These fake roses
They bloom
Then intrude

Bearing their thorns
That trick and lie
With satin, manmade leaves
Oh fake roses
How they capture
With beauty that deceives

So, which are you?
The real flower that blooms?
True to its roots in the earth?
Filling the world with real beauty
A quality of immeasurable worth

In this harrowing world of fake roses
You are the one of a kind
Where sameness and fakeness
Spans far and wide

Real flowers are hardest to find.

14. The Battle of Selves

Me.

Uninspired as blue fades to fire
The sun paints the sky crimson red
I sit, staring out
Torn into selves
A war raging on in my head

The battle between
A mind split in two
The duality of selves lashing out
Tug of war between chaos and form
A fight of both sureness and doubt

One self is certain
Positive
Free
She floats through life in bliss

But, self number two
Is negative and cruel
As wicked as it gets

Their weapons are words
That form into thoughts
Conflicting ideas plague my mental

The tension is building
My brain is in flames
This chaos unfolding
Demented

The clashing of selves leaves me breathless
Trembling
Weak in each knee
The dueling of opposites rips me apart
Two sides which will never agree

Stressed and confused
I refuse to take part
And so, I am forced to endure
To sit with this madness in silence
I remain irreversibly torn.

15. Out of Gas

I am a 95' Buick
I run on self-esteem
Chugging along
Stalling out
My gas tank is on E

Sputtering up a hill
With a gas station in sight at the top
The engine is rattling
Coughing up smoke

A roar
A gurgle
A pop

Persistent on the pedal
But the car moves in reverse
My mind, the reckless driver
Just making matters worse

My soul the silent passenger
Clutches to a map
Watching on in horror
As the car rolls slowly back

"We're out of gas"
But mind ignores

Suitcases of insecurities
Stacked neatly in the trunk
A backseat of anxieties
Unnecessary junk

"I'm throwing this away!"
Soul screams
"It only weighs us down"

Mind, the notorious hoarder argues
"I like keeping it around"

So down they go
Weighed down
They roll
Mind and soul
They fight

Now, at the bottom
Stranded
The gas station
Out of sight

Mind is pacing
Back and forth
"How do we make this thing run?"

Soul smirking stands up
Opens the trunk
"Glad you asked
This will be fun"

One by one, soul empties the cargo
Unloading each worry and flaw
Mind watches, while racing
Questioning itself
Confused
Intrigued
And unsure

Soul claps its hands in triumph
Sticks the keys in the ignition
The engine roars and comes to life
Now fueled by intuition

Soul becomes the driver
Proud behind the wheel
Mind, the happy passenger
They drive effortlessly up the hill.

16. The Porcelain Bowls

I was presented with 8 porcelain bowls
I wasn't quite sure what to do
So, I grabbed the first bowl
Poured out my heart
And then, I gave it to you

Bowl number two

Oddly shaped and awkward
As if cast from a broken mold
I toyed with it in my fingertips
And then, I poured out my soul

It reflected my image like a mirror
It lustered, embellished with gold
Since you already carried my heart
I gave it to you, to hold

Bowl number three, the biggest of all
Intricately adorned with a jewel
I poured in my mind
The liquid rippled
And like a fool, I gave it to you

Piece by piece
I took the rest of myself
And placed it in bowl number four
I handed it over, but your arms were full
So it slipped and fell to the floor

Distressed
I dropped to the ground
Tried to gather the scattered pieces
There's nothing in me and four more left
I sat there
Lifeless
Defeated

Wary with nothing to give
And every remaining bowl
Had I evenly split myself in half
You wouldn't have had too much hold

So it goes
If you give your "all" to someone else
And leave nothing for yourself
You'll long to be filled
Like the remaining four bowls
Left empty on the shelf.

17. Grammatical Massacre

Hidden moon
Dark room
In blackness of night
I turn
I take my words
Light them on fire
And observe them as they burn

The ink becomes ashes
The words become dust
They flurry to the floor like snow
My sentences succumb to the flames
I smile
Pleased, at this maddening show

Compelled to destroy
With the walls closing in
In the throes of grammatical massacre
Engulfed in smoke
Entangled in flames
The self-infliction of pain and disaster

Oh, how the mighty have fallen
These words that were once so cherished
I held them in, I held them close
Now I watched each line as it perished

The deed has been done
I'm greeted by doom
Consumed
By myself and their ashes
Incinerated literature
Meaningless embers
I weep, as I realize my actions

Dazed, staring into the cinders
Reality begins to set in
"What have I done to my words!" I bellow
As they lay there, lifeless and singed

Black hands
Crazed eyes
New perspective
Exasperated, covered in soot
Re-inspired by tragedy, self-inflicted
I sit down
And rewrite the book…

From memory.

18. The Unnoticed

It's everything else and in between
There but not
Unnoticed
Filling all the spaces of "what is"
Yet always out of focus

Lingering in the background of every scene
Much like a fly on the wall
A crack the brick
A chip in the paint
Faded writing on a bathroom stall

A dollar in the sand
A rare bird in the trees
And loose change lost in the grass
You'll find it
If you're looking
But usually
You walk past

The misfit insect
A silent spider
Hiding in the corner
He stays muted
The web he weaves is easily seen
Yet you still walk right through it

Hands in your pockets
Eyes to the ground
Footsteps silent and steady
Seeing only what lies directly ahead

Blinded
Distracted
Unready

Lift your head
Open your eyes
Glance around you

Look with intention to *see*

Only then will you stumble on life's little treasures

And all of its *unseen* glory.

19. Extinction of the Masses

The masses are captured.

Ruled by gears and coils
Machines that frame our minds
They shape our days
Swallow our moments
The slow wipeout out of mankind

How?

We fidget with our gadgets
Consumed by glowing screens
Caught in a perpetual delusion
And lost beyond our means

Nestled in our fingertips
A world that's always on
Severing connection with reality
Humanity
Now withdrawn

Victims of advancement
The innovation of demise
An extinction of the masses
Happening right before our eyes

Face to face communication
Now breeds dissatisfaction
As technology takes us over
Killing human interaction

What once was in our nature
Has slowly been erased
A hug, a kiss
Now emoticon
We've forgotten to embrace

Adapted to our gadgets
Creatures of machines
Losing sight of who we are
Obscene to me it seems
That the masses have been captured
By what's behind their screens

And so long as we consume it
It's us who are consumed
Human race
Now interface
Irrevocably doomed.

20. Morning Coffee

I have always been scared to say how I feel
The free bird who has broken its wing
Afraid to take flight after healing
Knowing full well how rejection will sting

But

I want to write you into my story
Scatter you into my days
Fall around me
Like confetti and settle
Surround me
Like a midsummer haze

I want to write you into my mornings
Watch the sunrise reflect in your eyes
Sipping black coffee
Lost in the moment
Staring out as the sun paints the skies

I want to write you into every sunset
Watch the sky
As blue fades to fire....
But here I am
So wishful
So scared
To admit this unbidden desire

Oh, shit

And if these words
Fall on deaf ears
I'll know, at least, I tried it
And continue down my fleeting path
Forever grateful our souls collided.

21. Reverted Streets

Two people

The regular city
Their common ground
Established gravel beneath their feet

Random souls
Two minds, inside lines
Drifting obliviously
They walk down the street
And never meet

Surrounded by ordinary streetlights
A row of buildings, all the same
Two passersby that never lock eyes
Trapped in their complacent game

Blending in with the crowds arounds them
Nameless faces that litter the scene
Walking on, heads down, unfocused
Useless cogs in a complex machine

Stripped of its magic
Flipped right side up
The inverted city is fading
The whimsical air has lost its allure
The twinkling lights, lose luster, abated

A chaotic mind burning fiercely
Looking on and never seeing
The amphibian-of-ambivalence paces in place
Searching the streets for a meaning

The city flips and it spins
Down the streets they saunter
Unaware, in un-fanciful strides
Walking along, indifferently
Two souls
On opposite sides.

22. Caged Soul

Remember me as you recede to normalcy
Natural order and ordinary flow
I only reside where the magic lies
So back inside I go

Oh no

Imprisoned in this cage of bones
Thrashing within the skin
Scratching at this bodily casket
Trapped from the outside, in

Tired of prying
I'm hopeless
I must settle with being confined
A wandering soul stuck behind walls
Of a realistic and logical mind

Coaxing myself for comfort
With intransigent understanding
The universe tells me the saddening story
That reality is far too demanding

Find magic in moments!
Find ecstasy!
A frantic search, there's much to be found!
I am a caged soul
Screaming for freedom
But body and life
Weigh me down

The world goes on around me
I watch through your dulled, glass eyes
Desperately searching the crowds
To find where the magic resides.

23. Magic of Madness

There is magic in the madness
You just need to know how to look
Hidden around you, sequestered
In every cranny and every nook

They tell you, "look on the bright side"
But anxious shadows are blocking your sun
And try as you might to sit 'till it clears
Your gut tells you to get up and run

You're restless and tired
Two things that compete
You can't find where your happiness thrives
So you run
In exhaustion
Searching for something
And eventually, the chaos subsides

Not all of it
Not none of it
But some of it
And for second, that's just enough time
To sit where you've stumbled
Slow it all down
Take it in, and finally unwind

A moment of rest
Blissful stillness
The world settles and freezes in place
You watch as a bird glides the skyline
The breeze gently kisses your face

Magic

These moments of stillness
Amidst all the madness
It's magic, right under your nose
The beauty in being so restless
Racing minds breed wandering souls.

24. Matching Strides

Two black shoes shuffle past
Dragging against the pavement
Footsteps heavy on the street
Avoiding cracks for entertainment

A blur of white, flashes by
Happily tapping down the street
Bouncing along in merriment
Each footstep, its own beat

They meet

Opposites attract, they say
And so, they fall in line
White and black
The perfect match
Four shoes that coincide

Corresponding pairs
With effortless, matching strides
Stroll along in sync
Their separate paces, harmonize

They part

A set of shoes slinks backwards
The other shuffles, swift
Pitter
Patter
On the gravel
Left and right foot, shift

No turning back or around
Just steady forward paces
Two sets of shoes
One white
One black
On their way to different places.

25. Granite Skin and Bone

An untouched slab of granite
One chip
My surface cracks
Incapable of being carved
You chisel
I collapse

On the floor before you
Lay my crumbled scraps
I cannot be sculpted
Nor fit the mold you cast

Yet, somehow...

You whittle at what's left of me
And slowly, I take shape
You carve a lovely curvature
One that I can't escape

You marvel at your masterpiece
A queen you've made from stone
But all you've done is trap me
In granite skin and bone

Imprisoned in this posture
Caged within position
I let you chip away at me
Inanimate submission

I hold my pose with dignity
As you hew me with precision
Defining all my features
But never asking my permission

A showpiece in an empty room
An object of possession
You chisel, chip, and scrape away
And shape my stone expression

Nothing lies behind stone eyes
I'm now your work of art
My outer stature—beauty
But my base a cold, hard rock

A sculpted slab of granite
Perfection in every part
But what you've left untouched
You never carved my heart.

26. The Hopeful Poet

Velvet scarlet curtains
A cloak that hides the scene
An empty theatre echoes silence
I slink back in my seat

Waiting for act two, scene one
A painstaking intermission
I tell myself "be patient"
But I can't help my wishful thinking

Such a hopeful play-write
I daydream happy endings
As if they'd somehow manifest
From an eloquent, well-thought sentence

Door swings open
Rusty jingle
A waft of coffee beans
I glance up at the door in hope
But it's not you, I see

My water-ridden notebook
Dog-eared and badly beaten
A pen that doesn't write that well
I sit there, half defeated

Waiting for a spark
The slightest strike of inspiration
But alas, all that I'm greeted with
Is handfuls of frustration

Such a hopeful poet
I dream of love and fate
But to me, they're only words I've written
To which, I can't relate

There's so much to discover
Behind the curtains, between the lines
This hopeful poet who writes her story
As the crowds file back inside

The scarlet drapes glide open
The paper hits the pen
She writes: "You, Me, and thirty-three"
Until we meet again.

27. Detached

Why do you cry? I ask her
The tears
Like pearls on her cheeks
Beads of sadness
Hit the floor
Sweet sorrows' bitter release

Why do you weep? I ask her
Awaiting her garbled response
But her lips are sealed
As are mine
Trembling with fear and remorse

Why don't we learn? I ask her
Her dangerous mistakes are my own
Trial and error
Over and over
A garden we've reaped and resown

Why do we falter? I ask her
Our curse of pure acquiesce
These instances from frozen lips
A maddening, twisted mess

But why are we crying? I ask again
Haven't we learned from the past?
As if she could answer
I scream in her face
But the concept is out of her grasp

Detached from myself
I plead with her
Why are we standing in place?
The streaks on her cheeks catch the sunlight
So I reach up to wipe off my face

Searching her eyes for hope, I ask
Are we going to be okay?
She nods her head
I sigh with relief
Then I turn
And I walk away...

From my reflection.

28. Spilled Honey

When seasons blend and flowers bloom
When endless night turns morning
With all my demons laid to rest
My heart still burns with longing

Filling the air like a dandelion
Set free by a gentle breeze
Floating
Up
Up
Up
And around me
All the seedlings of my dreams

Hanging on to moments passed
Like twisted vines that scale the brick
A flickering flame beginning to fade
From a candle at the end of its wick

Like muddy streaks and dusty patches
That cling to a windows glass
I grasp these distant memories
Clouding the present
With a mess from the past

Like a bee drawn to a flower
I linger on words, unspoken
I dwell on dialogues, bittersweet moments
Spilled honey from a jar that I've broken

Hanging on to all that was
Unable to let it just pass
I take a deep breath and wonder
Why only the good things never last.

29. The Mangled Quilt

I am sowing a quilt
The fabric
Erroneous assumptions
It's mangled, messy, and doesn't make sense
This quilt, embroidered with judgements

Threaded with expectations
From a spool of false conclusion
Woven with an opposite perception
Each patch, a well-crafted delusion

You see…

I've chosen the cloth with subjective lenses
The materials are rather deceiving
Random
Disordered
And senseless
But I am continually weaving

I thread an elaborate narrative
A quilted story
A desirable plot
My result has a favorable outcome
But unfortunately, reality does not

It's the sickest side of self-deception
The misconception of a moment
Because every story has two sides
And I can't sow that concept

So I weave this mangled quilt
Dissatisfied
Sloppy stitching
Then a scrap of fabric so true
Throws off my spurious knitting

Needle pricked fingers
Calloused hands
Exhausting repetitive action
I'm faced with the choice to finish
Or undo
Unweave
And refashion

Frustrated
Tired
Confused
I strategically grab the patches
Mapping them out to make sense of them
But still, the patterns aren't matching

So, I unravel the fallacious stitching
Discard the wrongful scraps
The product
A brand new quilt
Except this one
I've woven
With facts.

30. A Song Called Wrong

This all too familiar feeling
Alas, to be expected
The cruelty of "I should have known"
Again, I stand corrected

Laughing at myself again
Always, I find myself wrong
The words dance on inside my head
A timeless, well-known song

"All I have is me" it sings
"The lonely life that I've been handed
Floating along
Insignificant
I'll never understand it"

Always wrong plays on and on
A symphony forever repeating
The lonesome jingle, never ending
An ensemble so purely defeating

An eerie tune that fills the air
With unsettling instrumental
Verses consisting of all my false hopes
A refrain so detrimental

"You're wrong again, my friend"
It sings
Cutting through the silence
Floating around me tauntingly
In sheer, uncouth, defiance

I listen and I am befallen
Consumed by sad solitude
As the song always wrong plays on and on
And I become recluse

Where are you
Song of intuition?
You served me once, so well
But your notes and chords have left me
Stewing
In a wrongful songs hell.

31. The Scriptures of Intuition

Resting at the top of a shelf
In an upright, well-seen position
Collecting dust
Slowly decomposing
Laid my filed-away intuition

A leather bound book
With frayed edges
Decaying pages
Tattered and torn
Self-doubt is destructive
Eating it up
But to this, I say no more

Taped and glued
Barely holding together
Weathered
The binding is broken
A cover that's faded, protecting thin paper
Each word, unseen and unspoken

Long forgotten wisdom
Untouched words of peace
Scriptures of hope that lay weary
For a moment of long awaited release

"Take me down,
See my words,
Read my chapters!"
Desperate, it screams to be heard
Deafened by doubt, I ignored it
Haunted, by the cries of each word

No more
No more
No more
I resist my doubtful mind
I grab the book, open it up
Astonished by what's inside

Within the worn out pages
Written neatly in golden script
The answers to all of my questions
An elixir to my internal conflict

It sings to me songs of sureness
My soul waltzes along with the tune
I am a Phoenix, reborn from the fire
A butterfly taking flight from cocoon

A world once opaque now transparent
These pages have shifted my vision
Seeing myself through clear lenses
Freed from my own self-made prison

The weight on my shoulders now lifted
Embracing a new sense of self
Enlightened by the scriptures of intuition
I place the book of self-doubt on the shelf.

"Place the doubt on the shelf.
Face yourself."

Yourself.

Yourself.

Yourself.

Yourself.

Yourself.

Yourself.

Yourself.

Yourself.

Yourself. Yourself. Yourself. Yourself. Yourself. Yourself. Yourself.
Yourself. Yourself. Yourself. Yourself. Yourself. Yourself. Yourself.
Yourself. Yourself. Yourself. Yourself. Yourself. Yourself. Yourself.
Yourself. Yourself. Yourself. Yourself. Yourself. Yourself. Yourself.
Yourself. Yourself. Yourself. Yourself. Yourself. Yourself. Yourself.
Yourself. Yourself. Yourself. Yourself. Yourself. Yourself. Yourself.
Yourself. Yourself. Yourself. Yourself. Yourself. Yourself. Yourself.
Yourself. Yourself. Yourself. Yourself. Yourself. Yourself. Yourself.
Yourself. Yourself. Yourself. Yourself. Yourself. Yourself. Yourself.
Yourself. Yourself. Yourself. Yourself. Yourself. Yourself. Yourself.
Yourself. Yourself. Yourself. Yourself. Yourself. Yourself. Yourself.
Yourself. Yourself. Yourself. Yourself. Yourself. Yourself. Yourself.
Yourself. Yourself. Yourself. Yourself. Yourself. Yourself. Yourself.
Yourself. Yourself. Yourself. Yourself. Yourself. Yourself. Yourself.
Yourself. Yourself. Yourself. Yourself. Yourself. Yourself. Yourself.
Yourself. Yourself. Yourself. Yourself. Yourself. Yourself. Yourself.
Yourself. Yourself. Yourself. Yourself. Yourself. Yourself. Yourself.
Yourself. Yourself. Yourself. Yourself. Yourself. Yourself. Yourself.
Yourself. Yourself. Yourself. Yourself. Yourself. Yourself. Yourself.
Yourself. Yourself. Yourself. Yourself. Yourself. Yourself. Yourself.
Yourself. Yourself. Yourself. Yourself. Yourself. Yourself. Yourself.
Yourself. Yourself. Yourself. Yourself. Yourself. Yourself. Yourself.
Yourself. Yourself. Yourself. Yourself. Yourself. Yourself. Yourself.
Yourself. Yourself. Yourself. Yourself. Yourself. Yourself. Yourself.
Yourself. Yourself. Yourself. Yourself. Yourself. Yourself. Yourself.
Yourself. Yourself. Yourself. Yourself. Yourself. Yourself. Yourself.
Yourself. Yourself. Yourself. Yourself. Yourself. Yourself. Yourself.
Yourself. Yourself. Yourself. Yourself. Yourself. Yourself. Yourself.
Yourself. Yourself. Yourself. Yourself. Yourself. Yourself. Yourself.
Yourself. Yourself. Yourself. Yourself. Yourself. Yourself. Yourself.
Yourself. Yourself. Yourself. Yourself. Yourself. Yourself. Yourself.
Yourself. Yourself. Yourself. Yourself. Yourself. Yourself. Yourself.
Yourself. Yourself. Yourself. Yourself. Yourself. Yourself. Yourself.
Yourself. Yourself. Yourself. Yourself. Yourself. Yourself. Yourself.
Yourself. Yourself. Yourself. Yourself. Yourself. Yourself. Yourself.
Yourself. Yourself. Yourself. Yourself. Yourself. Yourself. Yourself.
Yourself. Yourself. Yourself. Yourself. Yourself. Yourself. Yourself.
Yourself. Yourself. Yourself. Yourself. Yourself. Yourself. Yourself.
Yourself. Yourself. Yourself. Yourself. Yourself. Yourself. Yourself.
Yourself. Yourself. Yourself. Yourself. Yourself. Yourself. Yourself.
Yourself. Yourself. Yourself. Yourself. Yourself. Yourself. Yourself.

Yourself. Yourself. Yourself. Yourself. Yourself. Yourself. Yourself.
Yourself. Yourself. Yourself. Yourself. Yourself. Yourself. Yourself.
Yourself. Yourself. Yourself. Yourself. Yourself. Yourself. Yourself.
Yourself. Yourself. Yourself. Yourself. Yourself. Yourself. Yourself.
Yourself. Yourself. Yourself. Yourself. Yourself. Yourself. Yourself.
Yourself. Yourself. Yourself. Yourself. Yourself. Yourself. Yourself.
Yourself. Yourself. Yourself. Yourself. Yourself. Yourself. Yourself.
Yourself. Yourself. Yourself. Yourself. Yourself. Yourself. Yourself.
Yourself. Yourself. Yourself. Yourself. Yourself. Yourself. Yourself.
Yourself. Yourself. Yourself. Yourself. Yourself. Yourself. Yourself.
Yourself. Yourself. Yourself. Yourself. Yourself. Yourself. Yourself.
Yourself. Yourself. Yourself. Yourself. Yourself. Yourself. Yourself.
Yourself. Yourself. Yourself. Yourself. Yourself. Yourself. Yourself.
Yourself. Yourself. Yourself. Yourself. Yourself. Yourself. Yourself.
Yourself. Yourself. Yourself. Yourself. Yourself. Yourself. Yourself.
Yourself. Yourself. Yourself. Yourself. Yourself. Yourself. Yourself.
Yourself. Yourself. Yourself. Yourself. Yourself. Yourself. Yourself.
Yourself. Yourself. Yourself. Yourself. Yourself. Yourself. Yourself.
Yourself. Yourself. Yourself. Yourself. Yourself. Yourself. Yourself.
Yourself. Yourself. Yourself. Yourself. Yourself. Yourself. Yourself.
Yourself. Yourself. Yourself. Yourself. Yourself. Yourself. Yourself.
Yourself. Yourself. Yourself. Yourself. Yourself. Yourself. Yourself.
Yourself. Yourself. Yourself. Yourself. Yourself. Yourself. Yourself.
Yourself. Yourself. Yourself. Yourself. Yourself. Yourself. Yourself.
Yourself. Yourself. Yourself. Yourself. Yourself. Yourself. Yourself.
Yourself. Yourself. Yourself. Yourself. Yourself. Yourself. Yourself.
Yourself. Yourself. Yourself. Yourself. Yourself. Yourself. Yourself.
Yourself. Yourself. Yourself. Yourself. Yourself. Yourself. Yourself.
Yourself. Yourself. Yourself. Yourself. Yourself. Yourself. Yourself.
Yourself. Yourself. Yourself. Yourself. Yourself. Yourself. Yourself.
Yourself. Yourself. Yourself. Yourself. Yourself. Yourself. Yourself.
Yourself. Yourself. Yourself. Yourself. Yourself. Yourself. Yourself.
Yourself. Yourself. Yourself. Yourself. Yourself. Yourself. Yourself.
Yourself. Yourself. Yourself. Yourself. Yourself. Yourself. Yourself.
Yourself. Yourself. Yourself. Yourself. Yourself. Yourself. Yourself.
Yourself. Yourself. Yourself. Yourself. Yourself. Yourself. Yourself.
Yourself. Yourself. Yourself. Yourself. Yourself. Yourself. Yourself.
Yourself. Yourself. Yourself. Yourself. Yourself. Yourself. Yourself.
Yourself. Yourself. Yourself. Yourself. Yourself. Yourself. Yourself.
Yourself. Yourself. Yourself. Yourself. Yourself. Yourself. Yourself.
Yourself. Yourself. Yourself. Yourself. Yourself. Yourself. Yourself.
Yourself. Yourself. Yourself. Yourself. Yourself. Yourself. Yourself.

32. Twisted Triumphant

Yourself.
It's the same thing that rips you apart
But can make you whole once again
One of life's most perplexing complexities
That turns your mind into a dangerous terrain

A dark forest that is ridden with creatures
Where your demons reside in the trees
Ready to pounce at the first sight of stumble
You walk forward, in shroud of unease

Menacing eyes trace each footstep
Your pace quickens
As you feel their wicked stares
The dark forest twists and turns
As you hallucinate
The first attack
You're presented with your fears

A valiant effort to entangle you in madness
But your soul is on a quest to be reprieved
To shatter the binding grasp of the shadows
A ceaseless battle, as you struggle for release

You break free

Trudging blindly through the vastness of the forest
You must face a final test to find the light
This battle is yourself that you must vanquish
The ultimate chance to advance and beat this plight

You're presented with your own wicked reflection
The evil entity of who you used to be
Taunting you with memories of pain and lust
But the armor you have built cannot be breached

You slash through the illusion of your past self
The demons shriek and recede into the night
You proceed down the path ahead
Victorious
Born again, as you crawl into the light

The shadows of the forest scream behind you
As you shed the tattered layers of your shell
You stare out into the heaven that awaits you
Having conquered every level of your hell

Saved from damnation by annihilation of the self
A righteous warrior emerges from within
A twisted triumph over all consuming evil
As it was written

The Good will always win.

33. The Symphony of Symbolism

Maybe I've gone crazy
Perhaps, I've lost my mind
I can hear the monsters laughter
Wicked
Cruel
Unkind

The beast has reawakened
From its peaceful slumber
Brought in reinforcements
And I am now outnumbered

A long awaited awakening
I should have seen it coming
Caught off guard and unprepared
Too tired to start running

So, I face them

They smother me with poisoned thoughts
Cloud my gaze with fear
I'm blinded by rain drops of doubt
A map that reads unclear

Oh dear

Into the ocean of chaos
These beasts have me surrounded
Maybe if I sink
I'll find safety in the darkness

But I float

I will not be defeated
Determined
I keep swimming
Although I'm growing weary
And my strength is slowly weaning

Thrashing in the crashing waves
Choking with each motion
These creatures have me captured
As they toy with my emotions

Breathless while I struggle
Yet, I know how to swim
So long as I can stay afloat
These monsters cannot win

I find myself on land again
Trudging through the forest
The demons chase behind me
Belting out a well-known chorus

Always wrong plays on and on
I
Am
So
Ambivalent
I'm out of gas and running mad
This darkened path seems infinite

I
Must
Re-main
Vigilant

Tripping over trunks and roots
Cut by thorns from plastic roses
Two selves run close beside me
Each one with different motives

They go unnoticed, before I know it
I am falling down

I am falling
Down
Down
Down
And then, I hit the ground

No sound

Repetitive mind is on rewind
No, not this time
I rise

Tired of their wicked games
Immune to all their lies

Bursting through the tangled trees
Into the path of the sun
I, the twisted triumphant
This battle of selves
I've finally won

As if waiting for this moment
For my soul to be at ease
On the ground before me
Is the puzzles' missing piece

I laugh
I cry
I write
This crazy, twisted story
Forming from every word before you

My glorious allegory:

Out of chaos.

11/13/19

I continually weave a mangled quilt
Not a victim, nor a creature
Stronger, having faced my truth
Now embracing the bigger picture.

Between the Lines

ENTERING CHAOS:
The Ambivalent Amphibians

November 13, 2018 was a crisp Autumn morning like any other. I was sitting at my favorite coffee shop before work, as usual. It was bustling with people and buzzing with conversation. The rustic smell of roasting coffee beans and fresh pastry filled the room. I was at the far end corner of the cafe, reading silently and sipping slowly on my cold brew. These were the simple pleasures I would indulge in every morning. Oddly enough, I was not enjoying them peacefully. I reached over to break off a piece of pumpkin bread, and suddenly felt squeamish. Everything froze in place. An unfamiliar shadow of uneasiness crept above me. I tried to make sense of my sudden discomfort, but my thoughts were a jumbled, racing mess. I felt the urge to run but I was stuck–glued to my seat, as if an invisible force was weighing me down. My heart was pounding erratically, my mind was racing, and I had no control over any of it. Then, a wave of unidentifiable panic washed over, crashed into me, and sent me spiraling into an ocean of mental chaos.

I was drowning.
In work, in my feelings, and in my surroundings.
I was overwhelmed by life itself.

And, I felt alone.

In that moment, I came to the frightening realization that I had no idea where I was, who I was, or what I was doing. I frantically searched for an answer but I found nothing. My intuition was gone. My heart was thudding wildly in my chest as if it was trying to break through my rib cage. I was lost, confused, and hurt. The coffee shop was full of people yet, I was all alone and so painfully unsure. The pipeline inside my mind had burst and every emotion came flooding in.

At this point in time, I was coming to the end of a dramatic weight loss, recovering from the sting of rejection, in the midst of unrequited feelings, and working 60+ hours a week. It was the grand show of my dissolving sanity, and I had nose bleed seats–too far away to understand what was happening, too far up to hear myself crying for help.

I was on a fast track, running full speed ahead, and I had finally come to a crashing halt. Indecisive by nature, I found myself falling deeper and deeper into a perpetually uneasy state about everyone, and everything. Nothing made sense.

Then, I came crashing back to reality. I glanced down at the book in front of me to distract myself from the startling emotions I had just experienced. In the middle of the page, in an ordinary paragraph, the word "ambivalent" glared out at me. It was as if it was demanding my attention. My vision blurred and the next thing I knew, I was writing furiously. The words poured out of me like hot, destructive lava. Each line burned down the wall of denial I had unknowingly been building–denial that my mental health was crumbling.

When I was done, I stared at the words in front of me. There was only one thing I was absolutely sure of: I was not okay. My veil of naivety had been destroyed and my "not-so-okay" mind-state, validated.

I had been in denial of "not-okay-ness" for too long. Why? I was always so used to having it all together. To me, not being okay was not okay. I was supposed to be positive. Optimistic. Glass always half full.

Alas, my mind had other plans.

Born from this place of pain, confusion, and realization – *The Ambivalent Amphibians* is my powerful self-reflection. At the time, it was the darkest thing I had ever written, a coming-to-self that I was drowning, and the gateway that led to my unsteady descent into chaos.

In the months following this moment, I lost sight of who I was completely. I was battling two sides of myself: the side of me that was logical and positive, and the side of me that was irrational and insecure. Half of me wanted to succumb to the madness and give up. The other half of me fought back, and I did everything I could to make myself whole again. I started going to therapy and he helped, but I knew this battle was one that I needed to conquer on my own. So, I dived into my own recovery. I read books about mental illness, I tried walking, journaling, and meditating. I ate weird foods and vitamins. I went to church. I drank Chinese teas and went to holistic doctors. I even got my cards read. I was my own project, a WIP (work in progress), engrossed in the great act of trial and error to fix myself. There were good days and bad days, but every morning I woke up and tried again. I refused to be consumed. Amidst this chaos, came *The Monster.*

AMIDST THE CHAOS:
The Monster

The Monster is the personification of my intrusive thoughts and the battle inside my anxious, obsessive, mind.

Monday, February 11, 2019. It was mental mayhem. My mind was an absolute madhouse. Why was I thinking these things? Where were these thoughts coming from? This is not me. I was sleepless and restless, running solely on caffeine and nicotine. At this point, I had not only lost myself, but I had completely turned on myself. Frenzied by these wicked, intrusive thoughts, I retreated. I ignored the world around me, afraid of people seeing that I was no longer who they knew me to be–that I was no longer who I thought I knew myself to be. I wallowed in my own false perception, believing my minds lies. I was trapped by my own thoughts, in mental anguish, and no one knew what was going on behind my eyes.

As I mentioned, there was a side of me that wanted to let the madness run its course and take me with it. Thankfully, my true self, the warrior within me, had to fight back. I fought inexorably against my thoughts as they festered. I labeled them "repetitive monsters"– ugly beasts that consume every part of the mind and cast a shadow over every part of yourself that you believe to be true. They are delusional mental critters, forcing you into the constant struggle between what is real and what is not. But that's not all, my thoughts manifested physically too. I was on fire. It constantly felt like there were hot coals piling on my chest, weighing me down. My breath was always quick and my heart was always endlessly racing. I was burning at my own mental stake, and feeling all the repercussions tangibly.

"Repetitive monsters" are wildly frightening. I questioned my sanity and my actions countlessly. If you've ever meddled with these fellows, you'd know that it can feel like there is no end to the insanity. The mental "compulsions" I used to ease the physical and mental burden of these racing thoughts became my psychological novocaine. They numbed the pain and confusion only for a moment, serving as a temporary fix, a BandAid. Then, a glimmer of hope when I realized I had found a way to conquer and silence them.

I realized this:

Your conflicting self, your anxious mind, your "anti" thoughts, or however you choose to brand these beasts, they feed on turmoil and fear. They grow stronger with every attempt of resistance. In order to rise above the relentlessness of an anxious mind, in order to release yourself from its chaotic grip — you MUST find peace in the madness. Sit with the chaos. Befriend the monstrous thoughts. Only then can you break the cycle, cut the chains, and melt the iron clasp that keeps you a prisoner inside your own mind. In order to regain control of your consciousness, you must accept its spontaneity. You must give in to having no control.

To win this battle, you must accept defeat.

After this piece, I completely stepped away from poetry. Anything I wrote became incoherent scribbling; a mess of my chaotic, repetitive thoughts on paper. Writing became nothing but a personal form of release. I put all efforts of writing a book on hold and convinced myself that nothing I had written would ever be good enough. I put the pen down, and continued to fight the internal battle with myself.

Time passed, seasons changed, and writing made its way back to me. I decided to compile all of my poems and prose together. The idea of writing a book was officially back on the table and it was a good distraction. The chaos was settling and *I was coming back*. Summer was approaching, New York City felt a little less gloomy, and as the flowers bloomed, so did I. Things were brighter and happier. I started enjoying life, noticing people, and finding magic in everyday moments. Ultimately, I began feeling like myself again.

As soon as I made the choice to write a book, the whole "falling into place" thing started happening. I began unexpectedly stumbling into strangers who all ended up playing a vital role in my poetic quest. One of those people was an artist. His work was not only phenomenal, but many of his pieces were reflective of my poetry. It was the first time I was able to connect the concepts in my writing with imagery. It's a funny thing really, my intention was to simply tell him how much I had connected with his artwork. I had no idea the impact it would have.
That's one of life's greatest lessons. The best people you meet are always unexpected, and always for a reason.

I believe that there is no such thing as coincidental interactions. Every one we meet serves a purpose; every one comes and goes for a reason. A good friend of mine once said, "People come into your life with a message. Either you have a message for them, or they have a message for you. It's up to you to figure it out." This is a statement that I have found to be indefinitely true.

Every person comes with a lesson. For me, when the lesson is learned, people fade away. My life is an infinite collection of fleeting interactions, all of which are wonderful and enlightening. Whether I like it or not, whether I try to stick around or not, fate usually sends me bounding around aimlessly, stumbling into strangers along the way. It's very exciting but again, painfully...fleeting.

RESURFACING FROM CHAOS:
The Fleeting Meteorite & The Inverted City

Wednesday, July 31, 2019. Summer was in full swing and I felt like myself again. I was reading a book about dark matter and there was chapter about meteors–which became the inspiration for *The Fleeting Meteorite*.

A meteorite is a meteoroid that survives the intense journey through outer space–first, passing through the atmosphere and then crash landing to Earth. The make-up of a comet is scientifically complex. It's full of big terms like "gravitational perturbations," "magnetic reconnection," "hydrogen cloud," and "ion tails." The point: there is so much more to the comet than meets the eye.

All we see when we look up at the sky is the beautiful aftermath of the meteorite's journey. As we glance into the abyss, we catch a glimpse of a shooting star. We see a sparkle, a spectacular flash, and experience the joy of this passing, glimmering moment. This galactic show is the comet's last hoorah, just before it loses its magnificent trail of light and crashes into the Earth.

The first part of this poem exemplifies the thrill and the short ecstasy of my energy–much like glancing up at the sky just as a shooting star is darting past. The second half is a nose dive into my shadow side. It's the part where I come crashing back down to Earth. *The Fleeting Meteorite* is meant to symbolize the yin and yang of a personality. The balance of both good and bad, sorrow and joy, chaos and form. It's the sadness of restlessness, and the happiness of being someone's shooting star, even if only for a moment*

One poem leads to the next.

While reading *The Inverted City* you may have caught on that it references two poems. You may have also realized that it tells a complicated story, and while maybe it's beautifully written, it doesn't really make sense. That's because it was inspired by a painting you haven't seen, a moment can never experience, and two people you will never meet. But that doesn't matter. Most importantly, this poem was the catalyst for the cadence of this book and it symbolizes my pivotal moment from "chaotic" to "poetic."

Aside from having imposters syndrome about my writing, I suffered from crippling stage fright. I refused to read my work to anyone. My words were my own, locked away, for my eyes and ears only. Sharing them was terrifying– mostly due to self-doubt, partly because of how personal they were, and always because of the fear of not being good enough. Crossing paths with the artist changed everything.

We watched the sunset and the moon rise from behind the sea of buildings. We talked into the late hours of the evening as we wandered the empty streets of New York, and stared out at the city laying upside-down. The streetlights were like a galaxy of man-made stars. The fountain on Park Avenue filled the silent city with its peaceful, rushing symphony. In that moment, I decided to finally read two of my poems: *The Ambivalent Amphibians* and *The Monster*. He was the first

*I'd like to give credit to whoever said "I'm a firework not a bonfire" somewhere in my life. I know I pulled that line from my subconscious, and one should always give credit where credit is due. Whoever you are, thank you for your words, I'm glad they found a place within my poetry.

stranger I'd ever read to and it was a big deal for me, especially reading two very personal pieces. The entirety of this moment was truly one of a kind. Afterwards, I was immediately re-inspired. In the days following that evening, I wrote *The Fleeting Meteorite.*

Soon after, he sent me a painting he'd been working on. At first I thought it was a twisted depiction of that night, but the more I looked at it, I wasn't sure what I saw. Naturally, I decided to write it out. When I put pen to paper, I had no idea where it would go, I just started writing a story. When I finally finished it, I realized that while trying to write the story that I saw in the painting, I had subconsciously weaved in my own. The poem became a symbolic mix of words that emulated my creative "resurfacing." In many ways, it symbolized breaking the chains of my reticence. After *The Inverted City*, inspiration struck like lightening. I hit the ground running, writing, and some of the best poems for this book followed suit. It was an unstoppable waterfall of words.

I bet you're wondering what happened next, but that's where our story begins and ends. It lives forever in the lines of that poem, and the inspiration from our transient interactions is undeniably sprinkled throughout the entire book. Simply put, if I hadn't met him when I did, this book would not be what it is. I don't know if we'll ever cross paths again, that's something I'll just have to leave up to fate; but I am truly grateful for having captured the story of the two people in a painting, two people in real life, and one beautiful moment in time. *To the Artist, Grant McGrath, thank you.*

REVISITING THE CHAOS:
Blocked & Grammatical Massacre

Once I decided to make poetry a reality, I fully immersed myself in the writing of this book. The time came when I was face to face with writer's block and doubt. Everything seemed to stand in my way and I questioned myself countlessly. Words felt like a jar of peanut butter on the top shelf–I could see them, but I couldn't reach them. The inspiration was slowly fading and as it slipped away, so did my sanity. *Blocked* was the product of this turmoil. It's ironic how the same thing that was driving me mad, saved me from madness. I wrote myself out of writer's block, but I was still battling myself. I had to make the choice of whether to proceed or quit while I was ahead. I chose to continue.

Boy, did that decision lead me down the path of destruction. Literally and figuratively. I came to realize that "chaos of the mind" takes many forms. While I had already conquered the beasts from the past, I was not out of the woods in the present. Anxiety and doubt began to manifest in new ways. They attacked the one thing that saved me, my writing.

I was consumed with finishing this book. Words took over my life. I was restlessly bounding around the city, writing in parks, coffee shops, and alleyways. The more I tried to force it, the deeper I needed to dig for emotional content. Since everything I write is based off my emotions, I knew I needed to explore the darkest corners of my mind. I had to re-live every emotional and influential moment in my life every time I sat down to write. Knowing this, I willingly accepted the challenge to dance with my demons in order to finish this book.

Let me put it this way, it was like I was throwing a dinner party and every demon I'd ever faced was on the guest list. Every single one RSVP'd. Every single one wanted a poem.

Each demon had a waiting seat at the table, their names written neatly on place cards in front of the plates I had voluntarily set. Anxiety. Doubt. Unrequited feelings. Fear. Loneliness. Ugly. Overweight. Not good enough. This was a party that I was fully prepared to throw, but I didn't expect the emotional disaster that would ensue shortly after. Halfway through the original thirty three poems, I had absolutely lost it.

Yes, I had knowingly re-entered the realm of chaos. I wrestled tirelessly with doubt. I started smoking cigarettes again. I dyed my hair from bright blonde to brooding dark brown. I spent all of my time writing, and kept to myself as much as possible during the entire process. For lack of a better term, I went mad. It got to a point where I hated everything I had written. I told myself it wasn't good enough and convinced myself that poetry was a ridiculous pipe dream. I was a fraud. Delusional. A bad writer. You name it, I thought it. I couldn't bear the insanity.

I wanted nothing to do with any of it. There was only one thing I could do to rid myself of it all–destroy everything.

Monday, September 9, 2019. The sky was black as ebony. A few whispers of light from the surrounding buildings slipped through the window and splattered across the hardwood floor. I sat crossed legged in front of the mirror, in the center of my bedroom, clutching the manuscript. Entranced by my reflection in the mirror, I reached for the lighter in my back pocket.

And then, without a second thought, I lit the manuscript on fire.

It was a slow, satisfying burn. I watched as the flames destroyed the paper, turning the words into meaningless ashes. The cinders stained my fingertips and littered the light speckled floor. I watched the lines disappear one by one, as the fire chewed at the edges of the pages. It was maddening. Exhilarating. Absolutely terrifying. It was the moment I had accepted the role of full-blown madwoman.

Then, a crashing force sent me hurdling back to reality. Clarity. In the act of this irrational destruction, I had an unexpected epiphany. The realization of the absurdity of my actions snapped me back into a logical mental state. I stared into the mirror, covered in ash, completely dumbfounded. After everything, how could I let doubt, fear, and anxiety win? How could I let my passion fall victim to my pain?

I had no idea what would come of this, but I knew in that moment, I had to see the writing of this book through. I was terrified. Fear was no longer the monster in my mind, it was now the fire at my fingertips.

Fear. The roaring blaze that blocks everything in your path. Another good friend said to me, "A true warrior never hesitates. You must make your move." He was right. Despite insecurity and doubt, you have to find the courage to proceed. You have to find the strength to face your fears.

I swept up the ashes from the floor and washed them free from my hands. Then, I sat down to re-write the book.

Yes, completely from memory.

After that, all the words fell into place.

Now, let's flash back to the beginning.

Out of

CHAOS

It all began with long, hard look in the mirror. I didn't like who I saw and I didn't know how to love myself for who I was. The girl I was staring at was overweight, unhealthy, and unhappy. It was time to change.

After 9 long months of radically changing my diet from junk food to health food, cutting my calorie intake significantly, quitting meat and everything sweet, plus hitting to the gym daily....

I had successfully lost 75 lbs.
I never thought I would write those words. Never.

Still, to this day, the concept is shocking. Losing weight is wonderful. You look good, you feel good, and people notice you. What most people don't realize is this: you can shed all the pounds you want, but you can't so easily shed the old perception of yourself. It's a dangerous mix of knowing you look great, but not being able to let go of what you used to look like. It's the twisted mess of not recognizing who are on the inside versus who you are now, on the outside.

I was battling with the false perception of myself both internally and externally. Physical and mental disembodiment. One day, I looked in the mirror. I stared at myself for what seemed like forever and I saw a beautiful girl. I stared at her defined features, thin legs, and slender arms. She was me, but she wasn't.

Who is she? I thought. Is she enough? Am I happy with her? Is she Natalie? Is she not Natalie at all? Can I be anyone I want now? I look different, therefore can I be different? Is she supposed to be more confident, because of the way she looks? Is she supposed to be happier? Less chaotic? Will people look at her differently? Treat her differently? Who is she? Who am I? Is that really me? Racing, irrational, confusing thoughts. When you've been staring into the same pair of eyes your whole life, your own eyes, to suddenly not recognize yourself is terrifying. What do you do when you lose sight of who you are? What do you do when you're not able to grasp the perception of yourself? I didn't feel like myself, I didn't look like myself, and I didn't know who I was. The girl in the looking glass was the same girl from the coffee shop–lost in total chaos.

In order to find myself in the eyes of that girl in the mirror, I had to learn. I had to let go of my insecurities, trust myself again and love myself for all my faults. I had to accept the madness and use it as motivation. Release myself from my own false perception. Befriend my monsters. Accept the chaos. In doing so, I found a strength within me I didn't know I had and I made a profound discovery: I was me all along, I just didn't know how to see myself for who I was. It didn't matter who I was from the outside, it only mattered who I was on the inside. That's who I needed to recognize. That's who I needed to heal. Truthfully, the chaos may never fully settle. But now, I know how to face it, to live with it, and handle it with my head held high. All of my monsters, are now my friends.

This battle of the mind, finding yourself, human connections, triumph, loneliness, sadness, restlessness, longing, hope, confusion, doubt – it's all part of this journey. It's all here, in the pages of this book, in the lines of each poem. It's me. It's you. It's us.

Dear reader,

I don't know where you are in your own journey, but you've reached the end of mine. Here is a final message I'll leave you with:

Never lose hope.

Remember, it is okay to not be okay,

Someday you will be.

Know this:

You can do anything.

You can be anyone.

You are stronger than you think

And greater than you know.

Most importantly:

You are enough.

This is it. At the end of this crazy, beautiful, mind bending journey out of chaos – I asked myself *one very important question*:

Who Is She Now?

Yellow shoes and purple curls
That girl
A walking rainbow
Glittering eyes of endless shades
Who's she? You ask, I don't know

Who is she? like a mound of clay
And yet, we cannot mold her
Perplexed, I stare at brooding eyes
And wonder how they smolder

Curls that bounce with every step
You try to match her strides
But she's too quick
Light on her feet
And so, right by, she glides

Who is she?
Loud and boisterous
A smile with a tune
Reverberating off the walls
Her laughter fills the room

Electrifying energy
Emitting from her skin
Who is that girl?
Who owns the world
And shines from outside in

Her vibrance is contagious
Bright-eyed and ever curious
Who is that girl?
Observing the world
As if it's not so serious

Head in the clouds
Arms open wide
As if to say "let's dance"
Who is that girl?
Her colorful world
Where all is left to chance

Who's she? that girl
I know her
Her eyes the same as mine
She's me, I'm her
We share a name
Two reflections

Now, aligned.

Change.

Special Thanks & Notes

First, the four important people: My mother, my therapist, my best friend and the artist. Thank you.

To my best friend, Colin Kelly:

Before all the chaos and weight loss, one person played a vital role in my life, my writing, and my mental health recovery. If it wasn't for him, I wouldn't be writing the words "I lost 75lbs." He endured hundreds of text messages, talked me through many bouts of madness, and was one of the first four people to hear my poetry. He inspired my weight loss and in many ways kept me sane. Like I said, everyone comes into your life for a reason and I would not be writing this now if it weren't for him.

To my therapist, Dr. Edward Black:

I was emotionally rising and falling with every single thing I wrote. I needed validation that they were "good." Every week, I was reading the new poems to my therapist. I relied on his encouragement to keep my doubtful mind at ease. He reassured me that my writing was adequate and kept me hopeful that completing this book was not just a pipe dream. Without these sessions, I never would have felt like any of it was anything of value (I may also have completely lost my mind by now).

To my Mom, Anita Nascenzi:

And lastly, a special thanks to the one who made me. If I could only tally mark all the times she said "print those out on the computer," I'd have about five full notebooks. Thank you for being there during all the restless nights, for answering my 3am phone calls, and for always encouraging me to keep writing. I would not be where I am today without you. I am truly blessed to have you. I love you.

In addition, a handful of wonderful people have influenced my poetic journey, my life, and have left an invaluable impact on my soul. Some of these people were fleeting interactions; people I stumbled upon, crossed paths with for a short period of time, and never saw again. I hope wherever you are in the world, that you're well. A special thank you to these people listed below:

Manuel Accimeus

Nick Belleas

Christian Clark

Nicolle DiIorio

Philip Erby Jr.

Lisa Lim

Emily McClarnon

Ms. McCusker

Bernard J. Nascenzi Sr.

Nathan Nascenzi

Leanna Stein

Matthew Wells

A poetic time capsule.
A diary.
Each story, a moment in time.

Periodicity is an important element in life and in the writing of this book. The mind is an ever changing landscape. How we feel now may not be how we feel tomorrow; our emotions are blurred as time ticks on. One day, the wrath of doubt may be all-consuming and so, the writing follows suit.

Another day might be positive, thus the words that flow have hopeful, happier, undertones. This life is an infinite collection of moments that we measure with hands on the clock and numbers behind the glass. As humans we are not only confined by time, we are also defined by time– captured by it, remembered by it, and guided by it.

I wanted to trap my poetry in the same way. Each one is frozen in the moment it was written and edited–documented by date, time, and location of inspiration.

The Ambivalent Amphibians 11/13/18 8:51am – Mad Men Coffee House
The Monster 2/11/19 22:19 – My Bedroom
Repetitive Chaos 6/23/19, 14:33, 8/18 15:44 – 1675 Broadway
Not Me 7/20/19 12:45pm – Brighton Beach
Nicotine Lust unknown – 571 Broad Rock Road, Front Porch
Who Is She? 7/28/19 15:30 – the church on 56th and Lex
The Fleeting Meteorite 7/31/19 19:00 – Sutton Place Park
The Inverted City 8/2/19 20:02pm, 8/2 3:58am – Park Avenue
World of Fake Roses 8/6/19 22:36 – Rose Garden at TJ Maxx
Path Of Sun 8/8/19 11:30am – East River Esplanade
Extinction of the Masses 8/8/19 8:42am – 53rd and 7th
The Rains Atlas 8/10 17:43 – 53rd street from Broadway to 1st
The Duality of Selves 8/18/19 17:20 – My bedroom
Morning Coffee 8/18/19 22:39 – My bedroom / Scarborough State Beach
The Twisted Triumphant 8/21/19 18:35 – Amtrak from NY to RI
The Unnoticed 8/24/19 19:53 – Sand Hill Cove State Beach
Blocked 8/28/19 21:00 – My bedroom
The Battle of Selves 9/2/19 19:44 – Clinton Cove / Central Park
Out of Gas 9/2/19 22:01 – The roof
The Porcelain Bowls 9/7/19 16:51 – My Bedroom
Grammatical Massacre 9/9/19 00:08 – The roof
Reverted Streets 9/9/19 22:41 – Park Avenue
Magic of Madness 9/10/19 18:47 – Andrew Haswell Green Park
Matching Strides 9/13/19 20:51 – 53rd street from Broadway to 1st
The Hopeful Poet 9/15/19 22:33 – West 86th Street
Detached unknown, 21:06pm, Broad Rock Road
Spilled Honey 9/21/19 10:33am, 9/22 14:28 – The roof
A Song Called Wrong unknown 18:27 – Central Park
The Scriptures of Intuition 9/29/19 10:55 – The roof
Caged Soul 10/13/19 7:50am, 10/16 20:37 – 63rd and 1st
Who is She Now? 10/28/19 12:12pm, 13:33 – 1675 Broadway
Granite Skin and Bone 10/29/19 23:07 – 53rd from 1st to Broadway
The Mangled Quilt 11/22 22:01 – The A train

About the Author

I'm Natalie. I'm 24 years old and live in Manhattan, New York. Originally from Rhode Island, I moved to the city in 2017 to pursue a career in advertising as a copywriter. I started out freelancing at a small boutique agency *drum roll please* and I hated it. I booked a one way plane ticket to LA and planned on kissing NYC (and copywriting) goodbye. Then, something magical happened–my good ol' friend fate stepped in.

The day before my flight, on the last day of my job, I was given the opportunity to interview at a different agency. Shockingly enough, they hired me on the spot and I started work that following Monday. Apparently it was just meant to be, and everything fell into place....and kept on falling.

Immediately after starting my new position, I embarked on a new journey–weight loss. Eight months later, I was down 75lbs. It all happened at once: a new job, a new life, and a new me. Learning to navigate a new city, a new sense of self, and a highly demanding job began to take its toll. This led me to my next journey, into chaos, which I like to call my "battle of selves."

This unexpected turn greeted me with crippling anxiety, intrusive/ repetitive thoughts, and depression. I was waltzing with my shadow self and dancing through life in total chaos. During this time, I was forced to face demons that I didn't even know I had, and the one true thing we all fear...myself.

Out of chaos came clarity, strength, and poetry; a new sense of self and a purpose–the completion of this book.

Through the lines of each poem, my goal is to make a connection with each and every one of you, by using words to convey this inevitable journey we all face as humans: the battle of the mind and triumph of the soul.

I have one single message of hope:

Out of chaos, we all emerge victorious.

Contact me at:
nnascenzi147@gmail.com

Follow me on Instagram:
@nncenzi